GRAVITY

by Robin Nelson

first step nonfiction

Lerner Books • London • New York • Minneapolis

Gravity is a **force.**

A force is a push or a pull.

Gravity pulls things and people to the ground.

Gravity pulls things down.

Gravity pulls leaves down.

Gravity pulls water down.

Gravity pulls apples down.

Gravity pulls a ball down.

Gravity pulls a roller
coaster down.

Gravity pulls a sledge down.

Gravity pulls sand down.

Gravity pulls a **yo-yo** down.

Gravity pulls
sky divers down.

Gravity pulls rain down.

Gravity pulls me down.

Gravity is everywhere.

The Leaning Tower of Pisa

Galileo

Galileo

Long ago, a scientist called Galileo did an experiment with gravity. The story says that he went to the top of the Leaning Tower of Pisa, in Italy, and dropped two balls. One ball was heavy and one was light. The two balls hit the ground at the same time. This showed that gravity pulls all objects to the ground at the same speed no matter what they weigh.

Gravity Facts

 Gravity pulls things towards the centre of the Earth.

 There is very little gravity in space. This is why astronauts float around in space.

 Your weight is the amount of force pulling you down to the ground.

 The Sun's gravity attracts the planets.

The Earth's gravity draws the Moon towards the Earth. Without it, the Moon would go flying into space.

 One story says that a scientist called Sir Isaac Newton first started thinking about gravity when an apple fell from a tree and hit him on the head.

Glossary

 force – a push or pull on an object

 gravity – a force that pulls things

 sky diver – someone who jumps from an aeroplane

 yo-yo – a toy that goes up and down on a string

Index

The photographs in this book are reproduced through the courtesy of: © Richard Cummins, cover, p. 10; Digital Vision Royalty Free, pp. 2, 22 (middle); Brand X Pictures, pp. 3, 22 (second from top); © Tom Stewart/CORBIS, p. 4; © Diane Meyer, p. 5; © Index Stock Imagery/David Davis, p. 6; © Brian Lawrence/SuperStock, p. 7; © Bonnie Sue, p. 8; PhotoDisc Royalty Free by Getty Images, pp. 9, 12, 14, 17, 22 (top and second from bottom); © Steven Graham Photography, p. 11; © Todd Strand/Independent Picture Service, pp. 13, 22 (bottom); © David Cavagnaro/ Visuals Unlimited, p.15; © Image Source Ltd., p. 16; Corbis Royalty Free, p. 18 (left); New York Public Library, p. 18 (right).

This book was first published in the United States of America in 2004.

First published in the United Kingdom in 2008 by
Lerner Books,
Dalton House,
60 Windsor Avenue,
London SW19 2RR

Website address: www.lernerbooks.co.uk

This edition was updated and edited for UK publication by Discovery Books Ltd., Unit 3, 37 Watling Street, Leintwardine, Shropshire SY7 0LW

Words in **bold** are explained in the glossary on page 22.

British Library Cataloguing in Publication Data

Nelson, Robin, 1971-
Gravity. - (First step nonfiction. Forces)
1. Gravity - Juvenile literature
I. Title
531.1'4

ISBN-13: 978 1 58013 367 8

Printed in China